Incredibly Easy
Gluten-Free recipes

Publications International, Ltd.
Favorite Brand Name Recipes at www.fbnr.com

Favorite Brand Name is a trademark of Publications International, Ltd.

Photography on back cover and pages 29, 35, 51, 99, 123 and 133 by Maes Studio.
Photographer: Mike Maes
Photographer's Assistants: Jillian McDaniel and Benjamin Stern
Food Stylist: Liza Brown
Assistant Food Stylist: Ashley Brice

Pictured on the front cover: Quinoa & Mango Salad *(page 36)*.
Pictured on the back cover: Flourless Peanut Butter Cookies *(page 122)*.

ISBN-13: 978-1-4127-8518-1
ISBN-10: 1-4127-8518-9

Library of Congress Control Number: 2008940483

Manufactured in China.

8 7 6 5 4 3 2 1

Microwave Cooking: Microwave ovens vary in wattage. Use the cooking times as guidelines and check for doneness before adding more time.

Note: This book is for informational purposes and is not intended to provide medical advice. Neither Publications International, Ltd., nor the authors, editors or publisher takes responsibility for any possible consequences from any treatment, procedure, exercise, dietary modification, action, or applications of medication or preparation by any person reading or following the information in this cookbook. The publication of this book does not constitute the practice of medicine, and this cookbook does not replace your physician, pharmacist or health-care specialist. **Before undertaking any course of treatment or nutritional plan, the authors, editors and publisher advise the reader to check with a physician or other health-care provider.**

Not all recipes in this cookbook are appropriate for all people with gluten intolerance or celiac disease. Health-care providers and registered dietitians can help design specific meal plans tailored to individual needs.

Contents

HOW TO EAT GLUTEN-FREE AND LOVE IT

What Is Gluten Anyway?

Gluten is a protein that is found in wheat, rye and barley. There are many reasons people avoid gluten. Celiac disease is the most serious. There are others who have a sensitivity to gluten and just feel better when they avoid it. Some people are allergic to wheat itself. You know which category you belong in if you're reading this book!

No More Bread? No Pasta?

At first, going gluten-free may sound awfully limiting. Fortunately, there are many more delicious foods on the gluten-free list than the forbidden list. There are also more and more products, from cereals to baking mixes to pastas, which are now being formulated in gluten-free versions. These days you'll find them not just in health food stores and online, but also on the shelves of most major supermarkets.

Some Good News

Spotting hidden gluten in processed foods is a lot easier now thanks to the FDA's Food Allergy Labeling Law that went into effect in 2004. Since wheat is a common allergen, any product that contains wheat or is derived from it must say so on the label. That means formerly questionable ingredients, such as modified food starch or maltodextrin, must now show wheat as part of their name if they were made from it (for example, "wheat maltodextrin"). Be aware that this ONLY applies to foods produced in the US and Canada. Imports are a different matter.

More Good News

Look at your dietary restrictions as an opportunity to try new foods. Add quinoa and chickpea flour to your cupboard. Use corn tortillas to make sandwiches or lasagna. You'll find easy recipes in this book that are so delicious you'll forget that they're gluten-free. Healthy eating may actually be easier without gluten, too. Adding more fresh produce to your meals, eating less processed food and avoiding refined flour are all steps to a better diet for anyone.

The Short List

Sensitivities differ from person to person and ingredients differ from brand to brand. Always check the label's fine print. This is an abbreviated list of some of the most commonly used items.

•Red Lights• (contain gluten)	•Yellow Lights• (check ingredients)	•Green Lights• (no gluten)
barley	flavorings and fillers	beans
beer	frozen vegetables with sauces/seasonings	buckwheat
blue cheese		cellophane noodles*
bulgur	marinades	chickpea flour**
cereal	mustard	corn
commercial baked goods	salad dressings	dairy
couscous	soups	eggs
durum	soy sauce*	fresh fruits
graham	*most are made with wheat	fresh vegetables
gravies and sauces		lentils
imitation seafood		meat & poultry
malt, malt flavoring and malt vinegar		millet
oats*		nuts
pizza		potatoes
pretzels		quinoa
rye		rice
seitan		rice noodles
semolina		seafood
spelt		soy
wheat		tapioca
*because they are processed in facilities with wheat		tofu
		*also called bean thread noodles **garbanzo flour

**Apple-Cinnamon Breakfast
Risotto (p. 12)**

**Crustless Ham & Spinach
Tart (p. 8)**

Cheese Grits with Chiles & Bacon (p. 22)

Cornmeal Pancakes (p. 18)

Smart Starts

Crustless Ham & Spinach Tart

1 teaspoon olive oil
1 cup finely chopped onion
2 cloves garlic, minced
1 package (10 ounces) frozen chopped spinach, thawed and squeezed dry
3 slices deli ham, cut into strips (3 ounces total)
1 cup milk
3 eggs
¼ cup plus 2 tablespoons grated Parmesan cheese, divided
1 tablespoon minced fresh basil *or* 2 teaspoons dried basil
½ teaspoon black pepper
⅛ teaspoon ground nutmeg

1. Preheat oven to 350°F. Lightly spray 9-inch glass pie plate with nonstick cooking spray.

2. Heat oil in medium nonstick skillet over medium-high heat. Add onion and cook 2 minutes or until soft, stirring occasionally. Add garlic and cook 1 minute. Stir in spinach and ham. Spread mixture evenly into pie plate.

3. Combine milk, eggs, ¼ cup cheese, basil, pepper and nutmeg in medium bowl. Pour mixture over spinach mixture. Bake 50 minutes or until knife inserted in center comes out clean. Sprinkle with remaining 2 tablespoons cheese. *Makes 6 servings*

Ham &
Potato Pancakes

¾ pound Yukon gold potatoes, peeled, grated and squeezed dry (about 2 cups)
¼ cup finely chopped green onions
2 eggs, beaten
1 cup (4 to 5 ounces) finely chopped cooked ham
¼ cup rice flour
¼ teaspoon salt
¼ teaspoon black pepper
2 to 3 tablespoons vegetable oil
  Chili sauce or fruit chutney (optional)

1. Combine potatoes, green onions and eggs in large bowl; mix well. Add ham, rice flour, salt and pepper; mix well.

2. Heat 2 tablespoons oil in large heavy skillet over medium-high heat. Drop batter by heaping tablespoonfuls and press with back of spoon to flatten. Cook 2 to 3 minutes per side. Remove to paper towels to drain. Add remaining 1 tablespoon oil, if necessary, to cook remaining batter. Serve pancakes with chili sauce.   *Makes 4 servings (4 pancakes each)*

*Tip

Rice flour can often be substituted for regular all-purpose flour in recipes like this one. If a small amount of flour is called for to bind ingredients together, rice flour works just as well as regular flour. Use either brown or white rice flour. Brown rice flour, like the brown rice it is made from, has a slightly better nutritional profile.

Apple-Cinnamon Breakfast Risotto

¼ cup (½ stick) butter
4 medium Granny Smith apples, diced (about 1½ pounds)
1½ teaspoons ground cinnamon
¼ teaspoon ground allspice
¼ teaspoon salt
1½ cups arborio rice
½ cup packed dark brown sugar
4 cups unfiltered apple juice,* at room temperature
1 teaspoon vanilla
Sliced almonds and dried cherries (optional)
Milk (optional)

If unfiltered apple juice is unavailable, use any apple juice.

Slow Cooker Directions

1. Coat slow cooker with nonstick cooking spray; set aside. Melt butter in large skillet over medium-high heat. Add apples, cinnamon, allspice and salt. Cook and stir 3 to 5 minutes or until apples begin to release juices. Transfer to slow cooker.

2. Add rice and stir to coat. Sprinkle with brown sugar; add apple juice and vanilla. Cover; cook on HIGH 1½ to 2 hours or until all liquid is absorbed. Ladle risotto into bowls and serve hot. Top with almonds and dried cherries and drizzle with milk, if desired.   *Makes 6 servings*

Smoked Salmon Hash Browns

3 cups frozen hash brown potatoes, thawed
2 pouches (3 ounces each) smoked salmon*
½ cup chopped onion
½ cup chopped green bell pepper
¼ teaspoon black pepper
2 tablespoons vegetable oil

Smoked salmon in foil packages can be found in the canned fish section of the supermarket. Do not substitute lox or other fresh smoked salmon.

1. Combine potatoes, salmon, onion, bell pepper and black pepper in large bowl; mix well.

2. Heat oil in large skillet over medium-high heat. Add potato mixture; pat down evenly in skillet. Cook 5 minutes or until bottom is crisp and brown. Turn over in large pieces. Cook 2 to 3 minutes or until both sides are browned. *Makes 4 servings*

Bacon & Cheese Brunch Potatoes

3 medium russet potatoes (about 2 pounds), diced
1 cup chopped onion
½ teaspoon seasoned salt
4 slices bacon, crisp-cooked and crumbled
1 cup (4 ounces) shredded sharp Cheddar cheese
1 tablespoon water or chicken broth

Slow Cooker Directions

1. Coat slow cooker with nonstick cooking spray. Place half of potatoes in slow cooker. Layer half of onion, seasoned salt, bacon and cheese over potatoes. Repeat layers. Sprinkle with water.

2. Cover; cook on LOW 6 hours or on HIGH 3½ hours, or until potatoes and onion are tender. Stir gently to mix. *Makes 6 servings*

Bacon &
Maple Grits Puff

        8 slices bacon
        2 cups milk
    1¼ cups water
        1 cup uncooked quick-cooking grits
        ½ teaspoon salt
        ½ cup pure maple syrup
        4 eggs
            Fresh chives (optional)

1. Preheat oven to 350°F. Grease 1½-quart soufflé dish or round casserole.

2. Cook bacon in large skillet over medium-high heat about 7 minutes or until crisp. Drain on paper towels. Reserve 2 tablespoons bacon drippings.

3. Combine milk, water, grits and salt in medium saucepan. Bring to a boil over medium heat, stirring frequently. Reduce heat; simmer 2 to 3 minutes or until mixture thickens, stirring constantly. Remove from heat; stir in syrup and reserved 2 tablespoons bacon drippings.

4. Crumble bacon; reserve ¼ cup for garnish. Stir remaining bacon into grits mixture.

5. Beat eggs in medium bowl with electric mixer at high speed until thick and pale. Stir spoonful of grits mixture into eggs until well blended. Fold egg mixture into remaining grits mixture until blended. Spoon mixture into prepared casserole.

6. Bake 1 hour 20 minutes or until knife inserted into center comes out clean. Top with reserved ¼ cup bacon and fresh chives. Serve immediately.   *Makes 6 to 8 servings*

Note: Puff will fall slightly after being removed from oven.

Gluten-Free Corn Muffins

1 cup cornmeal
½ cup sugar
½ cup gluten-free baking mix
1½ teaspoons baking powder
1 teaspoon baking soda
1 teaspoon salt
¾ teaspoon xanthan gum*
1½ cups buttermilk
¼ cup (½ stick) butter, melted
1 egg

Available in health food stores and near other gluten-free items in most supermarkets.

1. Preheat oven to 350°F. Grease 12 standard (2¾-inch) muffin cups or line with paper baking cups.

2. Combine cornmeal, sugar, flour mix, baking powder, baking soda, salt and xanthan gum in large bowl. Whisk together buttermilk, butter and egg in medium bowl. Add buttermilk mixture to dry ingredients and blend well. (Batter will be thick.)

3. Spoon batter into baking cups, filling almost full. Bake muffins 20 to 25 minutes or until lightly browned and toothpick inserted into centers comes out clean. Cool in pan 5 minutes; remove to wire rack. Serve warm.   *Makes 1 dozen muffins*

*Tip

Gluten-free flour mixtures can be found in the specialty flour section of most large supermarkets and in health food stores. They are a combination of different non-wheat flours and usually include bean flour (chickpea or fava), tapioca flour, potato starch and sorghum flour. Some blends contain xanthan gum, in which case omit the xanthan gum called for in the recipe.

Cornmeal Pancakes

2 cups buttermilk
2 eggs, lightly beaten
¼ cup sugar
2 tablespoons butter, melted
1 cup yellow cornmeal
¼ cup gluten-free baking mix
1 teaspoon salt
1 teaspoon baking powder
½ teaspoon baking soda
Blueberries (optional)

1. Combine buttermilk, eggs, sugar and butter in large bowl; beat until well blended. Combine cornmeal, baking mix, salt, baking powder and baking soda in medium bowl; stir into buttermilk mixture. Let stand 5 minutes.

2. Lightly grease griddle or large skillet; place over medium heat. Drop about 2 tablespoons batter onto hot griddle for each pancake. Cook about 3 minutes or until tops of pancakes are bubbly and appear dry; turn and cook about 2 minutes or until bottoms are golden. Serve with blueberries, if desired.   *Makes 4 servings*

*Tip

Most gluten-free flours and flour mixes should be stored in the freezer if you won't be using them up quickly. Store them in resealable freezer bags and allow the contents to come to room temperature before measuring and using them.

Wild Rice & Pepper Frittata

1 tablespoon olive oil
1 large shallot, minced
1 clove garlic, minced
1 cup chopped shiitake mushrooms*
1 large roasted red pepper, chopped
1 cup cooked wild rice
½ teaspoon salt, divided
¼ teaspoon black pepper, divided
⅛ teaspoon ground paprika
6 eggs
¼ cup shredded Asiago cheese

If shiitake mushrooms are not available, use any mushroom variety.

1. Preheat broiler. Heat oil in large nonstick ovenproof skillet. Add shallot and garlic. Cook and stir over medium heat 1 minute. Add mushrooms; cook and stir 5 minutes or until tender. Stir in red pepper, wild rice, ¼ teaspoon salt, ⅛ teaspoon black pepper and paprika. Cook and stir over high heat 1 minute until liquid evaporates. Remove from heat.

2. Beat eggs in large bowl with remaining ¼ teaspoon salt and ⅛ teaspoon black pepper. Pour eggs into skillet; tilt to spread over rice. Cook over medium heat until eggs are set but still glossy. Sprinkle with cheese.

3. Broil 3 to 4 minutes or until cheese melts and frittata edges are browned. Remove from oven. Let rest 2 to 3 minutes to firm up.

Makes 6 servings

Tip: To roast a fresh red bell pepper, place it on a stovetop over an open flame or 4 inches from heat in a broiler. Turn frequently to blacken all sides using long-handled tongs. Place the blackened pepper in a paper or plastic bag, shut the bag and set it aside for 30 minutes to 1 hour to loosen the pepper's skin. Scrape off the blackened skin with a paring knife.

Cheese Grits with Chiles & Bacon

6 strips bacon
1 serrano or jalapeño pepper,* minced
1 large shallot or small onion, finely chopped
4 cups chicken broth
1 cup uncooked grits**
¼ teaspoon black pepper
   Salt
1 cup (4 ounces) shredded Cheddar cheese
½ cup half-and-half
2 tablespoons finely chopped green onion

*Hot peppers can sting and irritate the skin, so wear rubber gloves when handling peppers and do not touch your eyes.

**You may use coarse, instant, yellow or stone-ground grits.

Slow Cooker Directions

1. Cook bacon in medium skillet until crisp. Remove bacon and drain on paper towels. Crumble 2 strips and place in slow cooker. Refrigerate and reserve remaining bacon.

2. Drain all but 1 tablespoon bacon drippings from skillet. Add serrano pepper and shallot. Cook and stir over medium-high heat 1 minute or until shallot is transparent and lightly browned. Transfer to slow cooker. Stir broth, grits, pepper and salt into slow cooker. Cover; cook on LOW 4 hours.

3. Stir in cheese and half-and-half. Sprinkle with green onion. Crumble reserved bacon over grits. *Makes 4 servings*

Goat Cheese & Tomato Omelet

3 egg whites
2 eggs
1 tablespoon water
⅛ teaspoon salt
⅛ teaspoon black pepper
   Nonstick cooking spray
⅓ cup crumbled goat cheese
1 medium plum tomato, diced (⅓ cup)
2 tablespoons chopped fresh basil or parsley

1. Whisk together egg whites, eggs, water, salt and pepper in medium bowl.

2. Spray medium nonstick skillet with cooking spray; place over medium heat. Add egg mixture; cook 2 minutes or until eggs begin to set on bottom. Gently lift edges of eggs to allow uncooked portion to flow underneath. Cook 3 minutes or until center is almost set.

3. Sprinkle cheese, tomato and basil over half of omelet. Fold omelet over filling. Continue cooking 1 to 2 minutes or until cheese begins to melt and center is set.

Makes 2 servings

*Tip

Omelets cook very quickly so make sure you have the filling ingredients ready to go before you start cooking the eggs. Don't think of omelets only as breakfast items. They make nutritious, quick, easy lunches or dinners and are a great way to use up small amounts of leftover cooked vegetables or meats.

Zucchini with Toasted Chickpea Flour (p. 34)

Quinoa-Stuffed Tomatoes (p. 44)

Socca
(p. 28)

Quinoa & Mango
Salad (p. 36)

Small Plates

Socca
(Niçoise Chickpea Pancakes)

1 cup chickpea flour
¾ teaspoon salt
½ teaspoon black pepper
1 cup water
5 tablespoons olive oil, divided
1½ teaspoons minced fresh basil *or* ½ teaspoon dried basil
1 teaspoon minced fresh rosemary *or* ¼ teaspoon dried rosemary
¼ teaspoon dried thyme

1. Sift chickpea flour into medium bowl. Stir in salt and pepper. Gradually whisk in water to create a smooth batter. Stir in 2 tablespoons olive oil. Allow batter to rest at least 30 minutes.

2. Preheat oven to 450°F about 10 minutes before ready to bake socca. Place 9- or 10-inch cast iron skillet in oven to heat.

3. Add basil, rosemary and thyme to batter; whisk until smooth. Carefully remove skillet from oven using oven mitts. Add 2 tablespoons olive oil to skillet; swirl to coat evenly. Immediately pour in batter.

4. Bake 12 to 15 minutes or until edge begins to pull away and center is firm. Remove skillet; turn oven to broil.

5. Brush socca with remaining tablespoon oil and broil 2 to 4 minutes until dark brown in spots. Cut into wedges and serve warm.

Makes 6 servings

*Tip

Socca are pancakes made of chickpea flour and are commonly served in paper cones as savory street food in the south of France, especially around Nice. Chickpea flour can also be used to make a thinner batter and cooked in a skillet to make a softer crêpe. Just increase the amount of water in the recipe by about ¼ of a cup.

Quinoa with Roasted Vegetables

Nonstick cooking spray
2 medium sweet potatoes, cut into ½-inch-thick slices
1 medium eggplant, peeled and cut into ½-inch cubes
1 medium tomato, cut into wedges
1 large green bell pepper, sliced
1 small onion, cut into wedges
½ teaspoon salt
¼ teaspoon black pepper
¼ teaspoon ground red pepper
1 cup uncooked quinoa
2 cloves garlic, minced
½ teaspoon dried thyme, crushed
¼ teaspoon dried marjoram, crushed
2 cups water or reduced-sodium chicken broth

1. Preheat oven to 450°F. Line large jelly-roll pan with foil; coat with cooking spray. Arrange sweet potatoes, eggplant, tomato, bell pepper and onion on pan; coat lightly with cooking spray. Sprinkle with salt, black pepper and ground red pepper; toss to coat. Bake 20 to 30 minutes or until vegetables are browned and tender.

2. Meanwhile, place quinoa in fine-mesh strainer; rinse well. Coat medium saucepan with cooking spray; heat over medium heat. Add garlic, thyme and marjoram; cook and stir 1 to 2 minutes. Add quinoa; cook and stir 2 to 3 minutes. Stir in water; bring to a boil over high heat. Reduce heat to low. Simmer, covered, 15 to 20 minutes or until water is absorbed. (Quinoa will appear somewhat translucent.) Transfer quinoa to large bowl; gently mix in vegetables. *Makes 6 servings*

Mini Carnitas Tacos

1½ pounds boneless pork loin, cut into 1-inch cubes
1 onion, finely chopped
½ cup reduced-sodium chicken broth
1 tablespoon chili powder
2 teaspoons ground cumin
1 teaspoon dried oregano
½ teaspoon minced chipotle chile in adobo sauce (optional)
½ cup pico de gallo or salsa
2 tablespoons chopped fresh cilantro
½ teaspoon salt
12 (6-inch) corn tortillas
   Cheddar cheese
   Sour cream

Slow Cooker Directions

1. Combine pork, onion, broth, chili powder, cumin, oregano and chipotle chile, if desired, in slow cooker. Cover; cook on LOW 6 hours or on HIGH 3 hours or until pork is very tender. Pour off excess cooking liquid.

2. Shred pork with 2 forks; stir in pico de gallo, cilantro and salt. Cover and keep warm.

3. Cut 3 circles from each tortilla with 2-inch biscuit cutter. Top with pork, cheese and sour cream. Serve warm. *Makes 12 servings*

*Tip

Carnitas means "little meats" in Spanish. The dish is usually made with an inexpensive cut of pork that is simmered for a long time until it is so tender it falls into pieces. Then the meat is browned in pork fat. The slow cooker makes the long, slow cooking process easy to manage and skipping the final browning lowers the fat content.

Zucchini with Toasted Chickpea Flour

½ **cup sifted chickpea flour**
1½ **pounds zucchini or summer squash (3 to 4 squash)**
2 **tablespoons olive oil**
1 **tablespoon butter**
3 **teaspoons minced garlic**
1 **teaspoon salt**
½ **teaspoon pepper**
½ **cup water**

1. Heat small skillet over medium-high heat; add chickpea flour. Cook and stir 3 to 4 minutes until fragrant and slightly darker in color. Remove from skillet; set aside.

2. Cut zucchini into ½-inch-thick circles or half moons. Heat oil and butter in large skillet. Cook and stir garlic 1 minute or until fragrant. Add zucchini, salt and pepper; cook and stir 5 minutes or until beginning to soften.

3. Stir chickpea flour into skillet to coat zucchini. Pour in water; cook and stir 2 to 3 minutes or until moist crumbs form, scraping bottom of skillet frequently to prevent sticking and scrape up brown bits.

Makes 4 servings

*Tip

Using chickpea flour to add substance and nutrition to vegetable dishes is a method adapted from Indian cuisine. The flour forms delicious, nutty crumbs that become part of the dish. The same method can be used with other vegetables as well.

Quinoa & Mango Salad

1 cup uncooked quinoa*
2 cups water
2 cups cubed peeled mango (about 2 large mangoes)
½ cup sliced green onions
½ cup dried cranberries
2 tablespoons chopped fresh parsley
¼ cup olive oil
1 tablespoon plus 1½ teaspoons white wine vinegar
1 teaspoon Dijon mustard
½ teaspoon salt
⅛ teaspoon black pepper

1. Place quinoa in fine-mesh strainer; rinse well. Transfer to medium saucepan and add water. Bring to a boil. Reduce heat; simmer, covered, 10 to 12 minutes until all water is absorbed. Stir; let stand, covered, 15 minutes. Transfer to large bowl; cover and refrigerate at least 1 hour.

2. Add mango, green onions, cranberries and parsley to quinoa; mix well.

3. Combine oil, vinegar, mustard, salt and pepper in small bowl; whisk until blended. Pour over quinoa mixture; mix until well blended.

Makes 8 (⅔-cup) servings

*Tip

While quinoa is an ancient grain that was grown by Inca Indians, it is new to most Americans. This tiny round whole grain is higher in protein than other grains including wheat. It contains all eight essential amino acids, therefore, it is considered a complete protein.

Thai Salad Rolls with Spicy Sweet & Sour Sauce

Spicy Sweet & Sour Sauce (recipe follows)
3 ounces thin rice noodles (rice vermicelli)
4 ounces large raw shrimp, peeled and deveined
1 medium cucumber, peeled, seeded and cut into matchstick pieces
½ cup fresh cilantro leaves
½ cup fresh mint leaves
1 large bunch green leaf lettuce or Boston lettuce

1. Prepare Spicy Sweet & Sour Sauce; set aside. Soak noodles in hot water 10 minutes to soften. Rinse under cold running water to cool; drain.

2. Meanwhile, bring water to a boil in medium saucepan. Add shrimp; return to a boil. Cook 3 to 5 minutes or until shrimp turn pink and opaque; drain. When cool, cut each shrimp lengthwise in half.

3. Arrange shrimp, noodles, cucumber, cilantro and mint in center of lettuce leaves and roll up. Serve rolls with sauce. *Makes 6 servings*

Spicy Sweet & Sour Sauce

1 green onion
2 tablespoons rice vinegar
1 tablespoon cornstarch
¾ cup water
¼ cup packed brown sugar
½ teaspoon red pepper flakes

1. Mince white part of green onion; cut green portion into rings. Reserve green rings for garnish. Combine vinegar and cornstarch in small bowl; mix well.

2. Combine water, brown sugar, pepper and chopped green onion in small saucepan; bring to a boil. Stir in cornstarch mixture. Return to a boil; cook 1 minute or until sauce is clear and thickened. Cool. Garnish with green onion rings. *Makes about 1 cup*

Buckwheat with Zucchini & Mushrooms

2 tablespoons olive oil
1 cup sliced mushrooms
1 medium zucchini, cut into ½-inch dice
1 medium onion, chopped
1 clove garlic, minced
¾ cup buckwheat
¼ teaspoon dried thyme
¼ teaspoon salt
⅛ teaspoon black pepper
1¼ cups chicken or vegetable broth
Lemon wedges (optional)

1. Heat oil in large nonstick skillet over medium heat. Add mushrooms, zucchini, onion and garlic. Cook and stir 7 to 10 minutes or until vegetables are tender. Stir in buckwheat, thyme, salt and pepper. Cook and stir 2 minutes.

2. Add broth; bring to a boil. Cover; reduce heat to low. Cook 10 to 13 minutes or until liquid is absorbed and buckwheat is tender. Remove from heat; let stand, covered, 5 minutes. Serve with lemon wedges, if desired.

Makes 4 to 6 servings

Variation: For a different flavor, add pancetta to this dish. Coarsely chop 4 slices pancetta, and cook in medium skillet over medium heat about 5 minutes to render fat. Add 1 tablespoon olive oil, then add mushrooms, zucchini, onion and garlic. Proceed with the rest of the recipe as directed.

Curried
Noodles

7 ounces thin rice noodles (rice vermicelli)
1 tablespoon peanut or vegetable oil
1 large red bell pepper, cut into short, thin strips
2 green onions, cut into ½-inch pieces
1 clove garlic, minced
1 teaspoon minced fresh ginger
2 teaspoons curry powder
⅛ to ¼ teaspoon red pepper flakes
½ cup chicken or vegetable broth
2 tablespoons gluten-free soy sauce

1. Place noodles in bowl; cover with boiling water. Soak 15 minutes to soften. Drain; cut into 3-inch pieces.

2. Heat wok or large skillet over medium-high heat. Add oil; heat until hot. Add red pepper strips; stir-fry 3 minutes.

3. Add onions, garlic and ginger; stir-fry 1 minute. Add curry powder and crushed red pepper; stir-fry 1 minute.

4. Add broth and soy sauce; cook and stir 2 minutes. Add noodles; cook and stir 3 minutes or until heated through.   *Makes 6 servings*

Tip: For a spicier dish, use ¼ teaspoon red pepper flakes.

*Tip

Asian rice noodles are a great go-to for gluten-free diets. Most are made of rice flour and water. Rice noodles come in various widths and are sometimes labeled rice sticks or rice vermicelli. Do check labels carefully, though, since some rice noodles have wheat flour as an ingredient as well.

Quinoa-Stuffed Tomatoes

½ **cup uncooked quinoa**
1 **cup water**
½ **teaspoon salt, divided**
1 **tablespoon olive oil**
1 **red bell pepper, chopped**
⅓ **cup chopped green onion**
⅛ **teaspoon black pepper**
⅛ **teaspoon dried thyme**
1 **tablespoon butter**
8 **plum tomatoes, halved, seeded and hollowed out***

Or substitute 4 medium tomatoes.

1. Preheat oven to 325°F. Place quinoa in fine-mesh strainer; rinse well. Bring water and ¼ teaspoon salt to a boil in small saucepan. Stir in quinoa. Cover; reduce heat to low. Simmer 12 to 14 minutes or until quinoa is tender and water is absorbed.

2. Heat oil in large skillet over medium-high heat. Add bell pepper. Cook and stir 7 to 10 minutes or until tender. Stir in quinoa, green onion, remaining ¼ teaspoon salt, black pepper and thyme. Add butter; stir until melted.

3. Arrange tomato halves in baking dish. Fill tomatoes with quinoa mixture. Bake 15 to 20 minutes or until tomatoes are tender.

Makes 8 servings

Asparagus-Parmesan Risotto

5½ cups chicken or vegetable broth
⅛ teaspoon salt
4 tablespoons unsalted butter, divided
⅓ cup finely chopped onion
2 cups uncooked arborio rice
⅔ cup dry white wine
2½ cups fresh asparagus pieces (about 1 inch long)
⅔ cup frozen peas
1 cup grated Parmesan cheese

1. Bring broth and salt to a boil in medium saucepan over medium-high heat; reduce heat to low and simmer.

2. Meanwhile, melt 3 tablespoons butter in large saucepan over medium heat. Add onion; cook and stir 2 to 3 minutes or until tender. Add rice; cook and stir 2 minutes. Add wine; cook, stirring occasionally, until most of wine is absorbed.

3. Add 1½ cups broth; cook and stir 6 to 7 minutes or until most of liquid is absorbed. (Mixture should simmer, but not boil.) Add 2 cups broth and asparagus; cook and stir 6 to 7 minutes or until most of liquid is absorbed. Add remaining 2 cups broth and peas; cook and stir 5 to 6 minutes or until most of liquid is absorbed and rice mixture is creamy.

4. Remove from heat; stir in remaining 1 tablespoon butter and Parmesan cheese until melted.
Makes 4 to 5 servings

Asparagus-Spinach Risotto: Substitute 1 cup baby spinach leaves or chopped large spinach leaves for peas. Add spinach at the end of step 3; cover and let stand 1 minute or until spinach is wilted.

Asparagus-Chicken Risotto: Add 2 cups chopped or shredded cooked chicken to risotto with peas in step 3.

Southwest Spaghetti Squash (p. 70)

Cajun Chicken & Rice (p. 66)

Gluten-Free Pizza (p. 50)

Rice Noodles with Broccoli & Tofu (p. 62)

Hot & **Hearty**

Gluten-Free Pizza

1¾ cups gluten-free baking mix
1½ cups white rice flour
  2 teaspoons sugar
  1 envelope (¼ ounce) rapid-rise yeast
1½ teaspoons salt
1½ teaspoons Italian seasoning
  1 teaspoon baking powder
  ½ teaspoon xanthan gum*
1¼ cups hot water (120°F)
  2 tablespoons olive oil
    Toppings: pizza sauce, fresh mozzarella, sliced tomatoes, fresh basil, grated Parmesan cheese

Available in health food stores and near other gluten-free items in most supermarkets.

1. Combine all dry ingredients in bowl of stand mixer. With mixer running at low speed, add water in steady stream until soft dough ball forms. Add olive oil and beat 2 minutes. Transfer to rice-floured surface and knead 2 minutes or until dough holds together in a smooth ball.

2. Place dough in oiled bowl; turn to coat. Cover; let rise 30 minutes in warm place. (Dough will increase in size but not double.)

3. Preheat oven to 400°F. Line pizza pan or baking sheet with foil. Punch down dough and transfer to center of prepared pan. Spread dough as thin as possible (about ⅛ inch thick) using dampened hands. Bake 5 to 7 minutes or until crust begins to color. (Crust may crack in spots.)

4. Top pizza with favorite toppings. Bake 10 to 15 minutes or until cheese is melted and pizza is cooked through.   *Makes 4 to 6 servings*

Fiesta Beef Enchiladas

2 sheets (20×12 inches) heavy-duty foil, generously sprayed with nonstick cooking spray
6 ounces lean ground beef
¼ cup sliced green onions
1 teaspoon minced garlic
1 cup (4 ounces) shredded Mexican cheese blend or Cheddar cheese, divided
¾ cup chopped tomato, divided
½ cup corn
½ cup black beans
⅓ cup cooked white or brown rice
¼ cup salsa or picante sauce
6 (6-inch) corn tortillas
½ cup mild or hot red or green enchilada sauce
½ cup sliced romaine lettuce

1. Preheat oven to 375°F. Brown ground beef in large nonstick skillet over medium-heat, stirring to separate meat. Drain and discard fat. Add green onions and garlic; cook and stir 2 minutes.

2. Combine meat mixture, ¾ cup cheese, ½ cup tomato, corn, beans, rice and salsa; mix well. Spoon mixture down center of tortillas. Roll up; place 3 enchiladas, seam side down, on each foil sheet. Spoon enchilada sauce evenly over enchiladas.

3. Double fold sides and ends of foil to seal packets, leaving head space for heat circulation. Place packets on baking sheet.

4. Bake 15 minutes. Remove from oven; open packets. Sprinkle with remaining ¼ cup cheese; reseal packets. Bake 10 minutes more. Transfer contents to serving plates; serve with lettuce and remaining ¼ cup tomato. *Makes 2 servings*

Pad Thai

8 ounces uncooked rice noodles (rice vermicelli)
2 tablespoons unseasoned rice wine vinegar
1½ tablespoons fish sauce*
1 to 2 tablespoons fresh lemon juice
1 tablespoon ketchup
2 teaspoons sugar
¼ teaspoon red pepper flakes
1 tablespoon vegetable oil
1 boneless skinless chicken breast (about 4 ounces), finely chopped
2 green onions, thinly sliced
2 cloves garlic, minced
3 ounces small raw shrimp, peeled
2 cups fresh bean sprouts
¾ cup shredded red cabbage
1 medium carrot, shredded
3 tablespoons minced fresh cilantro
2 tablespoons chopped unsalted dry-roasted peanuts
Lime wedges

*Fish sauce is available at most large supermarkets and Asian markets.

1. Place noodles in medium bowl. Cover with boiling water; let soak 30 minutes or until soft. Drain and set aside. Combine vinegar, fish sauce, lemon juice, ketchup, sugar and red pepper flakes in small bowl.

2. Heat oil in wok or large nonstick skillet over medium-high heat. Add chicken, green onions and garlic. Cook and stir until chicken is no longer pink. Stir in noodles; cook 1 minute. Add shrimp; cook about 3 minutes, just until shrimp turn pink and opaque. Stir in fish sauce mixture; toss to coat evenly. Add bean sprouts and cook until heated through, about 2 minutes.

3. Serve with shredded cabbage, carrot, cilantro, peanuts and lime wedges.
                                                    Makes 5 servings

Spicy Pork Chop Casserole

Nonstick cooking spray
2 cups frozen corn
2 cups frozen diced hash brown potatoes
1 can (about 14½ ounces) diced tomatoes with basil, garlic and oregano, drained
2 teaspoons chili powder
1 teaspoon dried oregano
½ teaspoon ground cumin
⅛ teaspoon red pepper flakes
1 teaspoon olive oil
4 boneless pork loin chops (about 3 ounces each), cut about ¾ inch thick
¼ teaspoon black pepper
¼ cup (1 ounce) shredded Monterey Jack cheese (optional)

1. Preheat oven to 375°F. Lightly spray 8-inch square baking dish with cooking spray.

2. Lightly spray large nonstick skillet with cooking spray. Add corn; cook and stir over medium-high heat about 5 minutes or until corn begins to brown. Add potatoes; cook and stir about 5 minutes or until potatoes begin to brown. Add tomatoes, chili powder, oregano, cumin and red pepper flakes; stir until blended. Transfer corn mixture to prepared dish.

3. Add oil and pork chops to skillet. Cook over medium-high heat until browned on one side. Place browned side up on top of corn mixture in baking dish. Sprinkle with black pepper. Bake, uncovered, 20 minutes or until meat is barely pink in center (160°F). Sprinkle with cheese, if desired. Let stand 2 to 3 minutes before serving.

Makes 4 servings

Roast Turkey Breast with Sausage & Apple Stuffing

8 ounces bulk pork sausage
1 medium apple, peeled and finely chopped
1 shallot or small onion, finely chopped
1 stalk celery, finely chopped
¼ cup chopped hazelnuts
½ teaspoon rubbed sage, divided
½ teaspoon salt, divided
½ teaspoon black pepper, divided
1 tablespoon butter, softened
1 whole boneless turkey breast (4½ to 5 pounds), thawed if frozen
4 to 6 fresh sage leaves (optional)
1 cup chicken broth

1. Preheat oven to 325°F. Crumble sausage into large skillet. Add apple, shallot and celery; cook and stir over medium-high heat until sausage is cooked through and apple and vegetables are tender. Drain fat. Stir in hazelnuts, ¼ teaspoon each rubbed sage, salt and pepper. Spoon stuffing into shallow roasting pan.

2. Combine butter and remaining ¼ teaspoon each rubbed sage, salt and pepper. Spread over turkey breast skin. Arrange sage leaves under skin, if desired. Place rack on top of stuffing. Place turkey, skin side down, on rack. Pour broth into pan.

3. Roast turkey 45 minutes. Remove turkey from oven; turn skin side up. Baste with broth. Return to oven; roast 1 hour or until meat thermometer registers 165°F. Let turkey rest 10 minutes before carving.

Makes 6 servings

Mile-High Enchilada Pie

8 (6-inch) corn tortillas
1 jar (12 ounces) salsa
1 can (about 15 ounces) kidney beans, rinsed and drained
1 cup shredded cooked chicken
1 cup (4 ounces) shredded pepper jack cheese
   Fresh cilantro sprigs and sliced red bell pepper (optional)

Slow Cooker Directions

1. Prepare foil handles for slow cooker;* place in slow cooker. Place 1 tortilla on bottom of slow cooker. Top with small amount of salsa, beans, chicken and cheese. Continue layering using remaining ingredients, ending with tortilla and cheese.

2. Cover; cook on LOW 6 to 8 hours or on HIGH 3 to 4 hours. Remove with foil handles. Garnish with cilantro and pepper slices.

Makes 4 to 6 servings

*To make foil handles, tear off 2 (18×2-inch) strips of heavy-duty foil or use regular foil folded to double thickness. Crisscross foil strips in spoke design and place in slow cooker to make lifting tortilla stack easier.

*Tip

Corn tortillas are an excellent substitute for bread in a gluten-free diet. If you have celiac disease or are extremely gluten sensitive, though, be aware that some tortillas may be processed in a factory that also handle wheat products. It is also possible that corn tortillas have been dusted with regular flour to keep them separated, but in that case wheat should be listed as an ingredient.

Rice Noodles with Broccoli & Tofu

1 package (14 ounces) firm or extra-firm tofu
1 package (8 to 10 ounces) wide rice noodles
2 tablespoons peanut oil
3 medium shallots, sliced
6 cloves garlic, minced
1 jalapeño pepper,* minced
2 teaspoons minced fresh ginger
3 cups broccoli florets
¼ cup gluten-free soy sauce
1 to 2 tablespoons fish sauce
   Fresh basil leaves (optional)

*Jalapeño peppers can sting and irritate the skin, so wear rubber gloves when handling peppers and do not touch your eyes.

1. Cut tofu crosswise into 2 pieces, each about 1 inch thick. Place tofu on paper-towel lined cutting board. Place weighted saucepan or baking dish on top of tofu. Let stand 30 minutes to drain. Place rice noodles in large bowl. Cover with boiling water; soak 30 minutes or until soft.

2. Cut tofu into bite-sized squares and blot dry. Heat oil in large skillet or wok over medium-high heat. Add tofu to skillet; stir-fry about 5 minutes or until tofu is lightly browned on all sides. Remove from skillet.

3. Add shallots, garlic, jalapeño pepper and ginger to skillet. Stir-fry 2 to 3 minutes. Add broccoli; stir-fry 1 minute. Cover and cook 3 minutes or until broccoli is crisp-tender.

4. Drain noodles well; add to skillet and stir to combine. Return tofu to skillet; add soy sauce and fish sauce; stir-fry about 8 minutes or until noodles are coated and flavors are blended. Adjust seasoning. Garnish with basil.
                                                                 Makes 4 to 6 servings

Italian-Style Shepherd's Pie

1 pound potatoes, peeled and quartered
2 to 3 tablespoons reduced-sodium chicken broth or milk
3 tablespoons grated Parmesan cheese
1 pound ground beef
½ cup chopped onion
2 teaspoons Italian seasoning
¼ teaspoon fennel seeds, finely crushed (optional)
⅛ teaspoon ground red pepper
2 cups sliced yellow summer squash
1 can (about 14 ounces) chunky pasta-style tomatoes, drained
1 cup frozen corn
⅓ cup no-salt-added tomato paste

1. Preheat oven to 375°F. Combine potatoes and enough water to cover in medium saucepan. Bring to a boil. Boil, uncovered, 20 to 25 minutes or until tender; drain. Mash potatoes, adding enough broth to reach desired consistency. Stir in Parmesan cheese. Set aside.

2. Brown beef and onion in large skillet over medium-high heat 6 to 8 minutes, stirring to break up meat. Drain fat. Stir in Italian seasoning, fennel seeds, if desired, and red pepper. Add squash, tomatoes, corn and tomato paste; mix well. Spoon mixture into 2-quart casserole. Pipe or spoon potatoes over top.

3. Bake 20 to 25 minutes or until meat mixture is bubbly. Let stand 10 minutes before serving.   *Makes 6 servings*

Bolognese-Style Pork Ragú over Spaghetti Squash

1½ pounds ground pork
1 cup finely chopped celery
½ cup chopped onion
2 cloves garlic, minced
2 tablespoons tomato paste
1 teaspoon Italian seasoning
1 can (about 14 ounces) reduced-sodium chicken broth
½ cup half-and-half
1 spaghetti squash (3 to 4 pounds)
½ cup grated Parmesan cheese

1. Brown pork in large saucepan over medium-high heat, stirring to break up meat. Add celery and onion; cook and stir 5 minutes over medium heat or until vegetables are tender. Add garlic; cook and stir 1 minute. Stir in tomato paste and Italian seasoning.

2. Stir in broth. Reduce heat; simmer 10 to 15 minutes, stirring occasionally.

3. Add half-and-half; cook and stir until heated through. Skim off fat.

4. Meanwhile, pierce spaghetti squash several times with knife. Microwave on HIGH 15 minutes until squash is tender (squash will yield when pressed with finger). Let cool 10 to 15 minutes. Cut in half; scoop out and discard seeds. Separate flesh into strands with fork; keep squash warm.

5. Serve meat sauce over spaghetti squash. Sprinkle with cheese.

Makes 4 servings

*Tip

If the sauce is cooked beforehand and refrigerated, the chilled fat will rise to the top and can easily be removed before reheating.

Cajun Chicken & Rice

4 chicken drumsticks, skin removed
4 chicken thighs, skin removed
2 teaspoons Cajun seasoning
¾ teaspoon salt
2 tablespoons vegetable oil
1 can (about 14 ounces) chicken broth
1 cup uncooked rice
1 medium green bell pepper, coarsely chopped
1 medium red bell pepper, coarsely chopped
½ cup finely chopped green onions
2 cloves garlic, minced
½ teaspoon dried thyme
¼ teaspoon ground turmeric

1. Preheat oven to 350°F. Lightly coat 13×9-inch baking dish with nonstick cooking spray; set aside.

2. Pat chicken dry. Sprinkle both sides with Cajun seasoning and salt. Heat oil in large skillet over medium-high heat. Add chicken; cook 8 to 10 minutes or until browned on all sides. Transfer to plate.

3. Add broth to skillet. Bring to a boil, scraping brown bits from bottom of skillet. Add rice, bell peppers, green onions, garlic, thyme and turmeric. Stir well. Pour into prepared baking dish. Place browned chicken on top. Cover tightly with foil. Bake 1 hour or until chicken is cooked through.

Makes 6 servings

Variation: For a one-skillet meal, use an ovenproof skillet. Place browned chicken on mixture in skillet, cover and bake as directed.

Two-Cheese Sausage Pizza Casserole

1 pound sweet Italian turkey sausage
1 tablespoon olive oil
2 cups sliced mushrooms
1 small red onion, thinly sliced
1 small green bell pepper, cut into thin strips
¼ teaspoon salt
¼ teaspoon dried oregano
¼ teaspoon black pepper
½ cup pizza sauce
2 tablespoons tomato paste
½ cup shredded Parmesan cheese
1 cup (4 ounces) shredded mozzarella cheese
8 pitted ripe olives

1. Preheat oven to 400°F. Remove sausage from casings. Pat into 9-inch glass pie plate. Bake 10 minutes or until sausage is firm. Carefully pour off fat. Set aside.

2. Heat oil over medium-high heat in large skillet. Add mushrooms, onion, bell pepper, salt, oregano and black pepper. Cook and stir 10 minutes or until vegetables are very tender.

3. Combine pizza sauce and tomato paste in small bowl; stir until well blended. Spread over sausage. Spoon half of vegetables over tomato sauce. Sprinkle with Parmesan and mozzarella cheeses. Top with remaining vegetables. Sprinkle with olives. Bake 8 to 10 minutes or until cheese melts. *Makes 4 servings*

Southwest Spaghetti Squash

1 spaghetti squash (about 3 pounds)
1 can (about 14 ounces) Mexican-style diced tomatoes, undrained
1 can (about 14 ounces) black beans, rinsed and drained
¾ cup (3 ounces) shredded Monterey Jack cheese, divided
¼ cup finely chopped cilantro
1 teaspoon ground cumin
¼ teaspoon garlic salt
¼ teaspoon black pepper

1. Preheat oven to 350°F. Spray large baking pan and 1½-quart baking dish with nonstick cooking spray. Cut squash in half lengthwise. Remove and discard seeds. Place squash, cut side down, in prepared baking pan. Bake 45 minutes to 1 hour or just until tender. Shred hot squash with fork; place in large bowl. (Use oven mitts to protect hands.)

2. Add tomatoes, beans, ½ cup cheese, cilantro, cumin, garlic salt and pepper; toss well. Spoon mixture into prepared dish. Sprinkle with remaining ¼ cup cheese.

3. Bake, uncovered, 30 to 35 minutes or until heated through. Serve immediately. *Makes 4 servings*

*Tip

Spaghetti squash is a healthy gluten-free pasta substitute. If you don't have time to bake the squash, follow the directions for microwaving it in the recipe for Bolognese-Style Pork Ragú over Spaghetti Squash on page 65.

Quinoa & Shrimp Salad
(p. 74)

Tuna Steak with Tomatoes
& Olives (p. 86)

Rosemary-Garlic Scallops
with Polenta (p. 90)

Noodles with Baby Shrimp
(p. 84)

Savvy Seafood

Quinoa & Shrimp Salad

1 cup uncooked quinoa
2 cups water
½ teaspoon salt, divided
1 bag (12 ounces) frozen cooked baby shrimp, thawed and well drained
1 cup cherry or grape tomatoes, halved
¼ cup chopped fresh basil
2 tablespoons capers
2 tablespoons finely chopped green onion
3 tablespoons olive oil
1 to 2 tablespoons lemon juice
1 teaspoon grated lemon peel
⅛ teaspoon black pepper

1. Place quinoa in fine-mesh strainer. Rinse well under cold running water. Bring water and ¼ teaspoon salt to a boil in medium saucepan over high heat. Stir in quinoa. Cover; reduce heat to low. Simmer 12 to 14 minutes or until quinoa is tender and water is absorbed. Cool to room temperature.

2. Combine quinoa, shrimp, tomatoes, basil, capers and green onion in large bowl. Combine oil, lemon juice, lemon peel, pepper and remaining ¼ teaspoon salt in small bowl. Pour over salad. Toss gently to mix well.

Makes 4 to 6 servings

*Tip

Forgot to defrost the shrimp? No problem—just place the frozen crustaceans in a colander and run cold water over them, separating them to help them thaw. Be sure to drain the shrimp thoroughly and pat them dry so they don't add extra moisture to the salad.

Lickety-Split Paella Pronto

1 tablespoon olive oil
1 large onion, chopped
2 cloves garlic, minced
1 jar (16 ounces) salsa
1 can (about 14 ounces) diced tomatoes
1 can (about 14 ounces) artichoke hearts, drained and quartered
1 can (about 14 ounces) chicken broth
1 package (about 8 ounces) uncooked yellow rice
1 can (12 ounces) solid albacore tuna, drained and flaked
1 package (9 to 10 ounces) frozen green peas
2 tablespoons finely chopped green onion (optional)
2 tablespoons finely chopped red bell pepper (optional)

1. Heat oil in large nonstick skillet over medium heat. Add onion and garlic; cook and stir about 5 minutes or until onion is tender.

2. Stir in salsa, tomatoes, artichokes, broth and rice. Bring to a boil over medium-high heat. Reduce heat to low; cover and simmer 15 minutes.

3. Stir in tuna and peas. Cover; cook 5 to 10 minutes or until rice is tender and tuna and peas are heated through. Sprinkle each serving with green onion and red bell pepper, if desired.   *Makes 4 to 6 servings*

Cheesy Shrimp on Grits

1 cup finely chopped green bell pepper
1 cup finely chopped red bell pepper
½ cup thinly sliced celery
1 bunch green onions, chopped, divided
¼ cup (½ stick) butter, cubed
1¼ teaspoons seafood seasoning
2 bay leaves
¼ teaspoon ground red pepper
1 pound raw shrimp, peeled and deveined
5⅓ cups water
1⅓ cups quick-cooking grits
2 cups (8 ounces) shredded sharp Cheddar cheese
¼ cup whipping cream or half-and-half

Slow Cooker Directions

1. Coat slow cooker with nonstick cooking spray. Add bell peppers, celery, half of green onions, butter, seafood seasoning, bay leaves and red pepper. Cover; cook on LOW 4 hours or on HIGH 2 hours.

2. *Turn slow cooker to HIGH.* Add shrimp. Cover; cook 15 minutes. Meanwhile, bring water to a boil in medium saucepan. Add grits and cook according to directions on package.

3. Discard bay leaves. Stir cheese, cream and remaining green onions into slow cooker. Cook 5 minutes or until cheese melts. Serve over grits.

Makes 6 servings

Variation: This dish is also delicious served over polenta.

Pecan Catfish with Cranberry Compote

Cranberry Compote (recipe follows)
1½ cups pecans
2 tablespoons rice flour
1 egg
2 tablespoons water
Salt and pepper
4 catfish fillets (about 1¼ pounds)
2 tablespoons butter, divided

1. Prepare Cranberry Compote and refrigerate at least 3 hours or up to several days ahead.

2. Preheat oven to 425°F. Place pecans and rice flour in bowl of food processor; pulse just until finely chopped. *Do not overprocess.* Place pecan mixture in shallow dish or plate. Whisk egg and water in another shallow dish. Sprinkle salt and pepper on both sides of each fillet; dip in egg, then in pecan mixture, pressing to make coating stick.

3. Place 1 tablespoon butter in 13×9-inch baking pan. Melt butter on stovetop or in oven and tilt pan to distribute evenly.

4. Place fillets in prepared pan in single layer. Dot with remaining 1 tablespoon butter. Bake 15 to 20 minutes or until fish begins to flake when tested with fork. Serve with Cranberry Compote.

Makes 4 servings

Cranberry Compote

1 package (12 ounces) cranberries
¾ cup water
⅔ cup sugar
¼ cup orange juice
2 teaspoons grated fresh ginger
¼ teaspoon five-spice powder
⅛ teaspoon salt
1 teaspoon butter

continued on page 82

Cranberry Compote, continued

1. Wash and pick over cranberries, discarding any bad ones. Combine cranberries and all remaining ingredients except butter in large saucepan. Heat over medium-high heat, stirring occasionally, about 10 minutes or until berries begin to pop.

2. Cook and stir 5 minutes or until saucy consistency is reached. Remove from heat; stir in butter. Allow to cool; refrigerate until cold. Compote can be stored up to 1 week in refrigerator. *Makes 2 cups*

Roasted Almond Tilapia

2 tilapia or Boston scrod fillets (6 ounces each)
¼ teaspoon salt
1 tablespoon prepared mustard
¼ cup rice flour
2 tablespoons chopped almonds
Paprika (optional)
Lemon wedges

1. Preheat oven to 450°F. Place fish on small baking sheet; season with salt. Spread mustard over fish. Combine rice flour and almonds in small bowl; sprinkle over fish. Press lightly to adhere. Sprinkle with paprika, if desired.

2. Bake 8 to 10 minutes or until fish is opaque in center and begins to flake when tested with fork. Serve with lemon wedges, if desired.
Makes 2 servings

Noodles with Baby Shrimp

1 package (3¾ ounces) cellophane noodles
3 green onions
1 tablespoon vegetable oil
1 package (16 ounces) frozen mixed vegetables (such as cauliflower, broccoli and carrots)
1 cup vegetable broth
8 ounces cooked frozen baby shrimp
1 tablespoon gluten-free soy sauce
2 teaspoons dark sesame oil
¼ teaspoon black pepper

1. Place noodles in large bowl. Cover with boiling water; let soak 10 to 15 minutes or just until softened. Drain noodles. Cut noodles into 5- or 6-inch pieces; set aside. Cut green onions into 1-inch pieces.

2. Heat wok or large skillet over high heat about 1 minute or until hot. Drizzle vegetable oil into wok; heat 30 seconds. Add green onions; stir-fry 1 minute. Add mixed vegetables; stir-fry 2 minutes. Add broth; bring to a boil. Reduce heat to low; cover and cook 5 minutes or until vegetables are crisp-tender.

3. Add shrimp to wok; cook just until thawed. Stir in noodles, soy sauce, sesame oil and pepper; stir-fry until heated through.

Makes 4 to 6 servings

*Tip

Cellophane noodles are also called bean thread noodles or glass noodles. These clear, thin noodles are made from mung bean starch and so are gluten-free. They are sold in packages of 6 to 8 tangled bunches in the Asian section of the supermarket.

Tuna Steaks with Tomatoes & Olives

2 teaspoons olive oil
1 small onion, quartered and sliced
1 clove garlic, minced
1⅓ cups chopped tomatoes
¼ cup sliced drained black olives
2 anchovy fillets, finely chopped (optional)
2 tablespoons chopped fresh basil
¼ teaspoon salt, divided
⅛ teaspoon red pepper flakes
4 tuna steaks (¾ inch thick)
Black pepper
Nonstick cooking spray
¼ cup toasted pine nuts

1. Heat oil in large skillet over medium heat. Add onion; cook and stir 4 minutes. Add garlic; cook and stir about 30 seconds. Add tomatoes; cook 3 minutes, stirring occasionally. Stir in olives, anchovies, if desired, basil, ⅛ teaspoon salt and red pepper flakes. Cook until most of liquid is evaporated.

2. Meanwhile, sprinkle tuna with remaining ⅛ teaspoon salt and black pepper. Spray large nonstick skillet with cooking spray; heat over medium-high heat. Cook tuna 2 minutes on each side for medium-rare or until desired doneness. Serve with tomato mixture. Sprinkle with pine nuts.

Makes 4 servings

*Tip

To toast pine nuts, place them in a small, dry skillet over medium-low heat. Cook, stirring occasionally, 3 to 5 minutes or until the nuts are fragrant and golden. Watch closely since pine nuts scorch easily.

Fast Catfish in Foil

4 catfish fillets
2 cups shredded carrots
6 ounces green beans, ends trimmed (about 60 beans)
8 unpeeled baby red potatoes, thinly sliced
   Nonstick cooking spray
4 teaspoons lemon juice
2 teaspoons dried parsley flakes
   Salt and black pepper

1. Preheat oven to 425°F. Place one fillet, skin side down, on each of 4 (12×12-inch) sheets of foil. Top each fillet with one fourth of carrots, green beans and sliced potatoes.

2. Spray ingredients on each foil square with cooking spray. Sprinkle each with lemon juice and parsley flakes. Season with salt and pepper.

3. Fold foil into packets. Place packets on baking sheet. Bake 15 to 30 minutes or until fish is cooked through and vegetables are tender. Remove packets from oven; let stand 5 minutes. Carefully open packets, allowing steam to escape. *Makes 4 servings*

Hazelnut-Coated Salmon Steaks

¼ cup hazelnuts
4 salmon steaks (about 5 ounces each)
1 tablespoon apple butter
1 tablespoon Dijon mustard
¼ teaspoon dried thyme
⅛ teaspoon black pepper

1. Preheat oven to 375°F. Place hazelnuts on baking sheet; bake 8 minutes or until fragrant. Quickly transfer nuts to clean dry dish towel. Fold towel; rub vigorously to remove skins. Finely chop hazelnuts.

2. *Increase oven temperature to 450°F.* Place salmon in baking dish. Combine apple butter, mustard, thyme and pepper in small bowl. Brush on salmon; top with nuts. Bake 14 to 16 minutes or until fish begins to flake when tested with fork. *Makes 4 servings*

Serving Suggestion: Steamed rice and snow peas are the perfect accompaniments to these flavorful salmon steaks.

Greek-Style Salmon

1½ teaspoons olive oil
1¾ cups diced tomatoes, drained
  6 black olives, coarsely chopped
  4 green olives, coarsely chopped
  3 tablespoons lemon juice
  2 tablespoons chopped fresh Italian parsley
  1 tablespoon capers, rinsed and drained
  2 cloves garlic, thinly sliced
  ¼ teaspoon black pepper
  1 pound salmon fillets

1. Heat oil in large skillet over medium-high heat. Add tomatoes, olives, lemon juice, parsley, capers, garlic and pepper; bring to a boil over medium heat, stirring frequently.

2. Cook tomato mixture 5 minutes or until reduced by about one third, stirring occasionally.

3. Rinse salmon and pat dry with paper towels. Push sauce to one side of skillet. Add salmon to skillet; spoon sauce over salmon. Cover and cook 15 minutes or until salmon begins to flake when tested with fork.

Makes 4 servings

Rosemary-Garlic Scallops with Polenta

2 teaspoons olive oil
1 medium red bell pepper, sliced
⅓ cup chopped red onion
3 cloves garlic, minced
½ pound fresh bay scallops
2 teaspoons chopped fresh rosemary *or* **¾ teaspoon dried rosemary**
¼ teaspoon black pepper
1¼ cups reduced-sodium chicken broth
½ cup cornmeal
¼ teaspoon salt

1. Heat oil in large nonstick skillet over medium heat. Add bell pepper, onion and garlic. Cook and stir 5 minutes. Add scallops, rosemary and black pepper. Cook 3 to 5 minutes or until scallops are opaque, stirring occasionally.

2. Meanwhile, combine broth, cornmeal and salt in small saucepan. Bring to a boil over high heat. Reduce heat to low; simmer 5 minutes or until polenta is very thick, stirring frequently. Transfer to two serving plates. Top polenta with scallop mixture. *Makes 2 servings*

Salmon-Potato Cakes with Mustard Tartar Sauce

Salmon-Potato Cakes
  3 small unpeeled red potatoes (8 ounces)
  1 cup cooked flaked salmon
  1 egg white
  2 green onions, chopped
  1 tablespoon chopped fresh parsley
  ½ teaspoon Cajun seasoning
  1 teaspoon olive oil

Mustard Tartar Sauce
  1 tablespoon mayonnaise
  1 tablespoon plain yogurt or sour cream
  2 teaspoons coarse grain mustard
  1 tablespoon chopped fresh parsley
  1 tablespoon chopped dill pickle
  1 teaspoon lemon juice

1. Halve potatoes; place in small saucepan. Cover with water; bring to a boil. Reduce heat and simmer until potatoes are tender, about 15 minutes. Drain. Mash potatoes with fork, leaving chunky texture.

2. Combine mashed potatoes, salmon, egg white, green onions, parsley and seasoning in medium bowl.

3. Heat oil in nonstick skillet over medium heat. Shape salmon mixture into 2 patties; place in skillet. Flatten slightly. Cook 7 minutes or until browned, turning halfway through cooking time.

4. Meanwhile, combine sauce ingredients in small bowl. Serve with cakes.
Makes 2 servings

Grilled
Fish Tacos

¾ teaspoon chili powder
1 pound skinless mahi mahi, halibut or tilapia fillets
½ cup salsa, divided
2 cups shredded cabbage or packaged cole slaw mix
¼ cup sour cream
¼ cup chopped fresh cilantro, divided
8 (6-inch) corn tortillas, warmed

1. Prepare grill for direct cooking. Sprinkle chili powder over fish. Spoon ¼ cup salsa over fish; let stand 10 minutes. Meanwhile, combine cabbage, remaining ¼ cup salsa, sour cream and 2 tablespoons cilantro in large bowl; mix well.

2. Grill fish, covered, over medium heat 8 to 10 minutes without turning or until fish begins to flake when tested with fork. Break fish into bite-size chunks. Fill tortillas with fish and cabbage mixture. Garnish with remaining cilantro.   *Makes 4 servings*

*Tip

Most chili powders and spice mixes are gluten-free, but it's still a good idea to check the ingredients label to make sure there are no hidden problems. Fortunately with the new labeling laws, formerly suspect ingredients, such as maltodextrin, now have to list wheat if they are made from it.

**Flourless Fried Chicken
Tenders (p. 98)**

**Cornish Hens with Wild Rice
& Pine Nut Pilaf (p. 100)**

Indian-Style Apricot Chicken (p. 104)

Turkey with Pecan-Cherry Stuffing (p. 106)

Better **Birds**

Flourless Fried Chicken Tenders

1½ cups chickpea flour*
1½ teaspoons Italian seasoning
 1 teaspoon salt
 ½ teaspoon black pepper
 ⅛ teaspoon ground red pepper
 ¾ cup plus 2 to 4 tablespoons water
    Oil for frying
 1 pound chicken tenders, cut in half if large
    Curry Mayo Dipping Sauce (optional)

Chickpea flour is also called garbanzo flour. It is found in the specialty food section of most supermarkets.

1. Sift chickpea flour into medium bowl. Stir in Italian seasoning, salt, black pepper and red pepper. Gradually whisk in ¾ cup water to make smooth batter. Whisk in additional water by tablespoons if needed until batter is consistency of heavy cream.

2. Meanwhile, add oil to large heavy skillet or Dutch oven to ¾-inch depth. Heat over medium-high heat until drop of batter placed in oil sizzles (350°F).

3. Pat chicken pieces dry. Dip chicken into batter with tongs; let excess fall back into bowl. Ease chicken gently into oil; fry 2 to 3 minutes per side until slightly browned and chicken is cooked through. Fry in batches; do not crowd pan.

4. Drain chicken on paper towels. Serve warm with Curry Mayo Dipping Sauce, if desired.   *Makes 4 servings*

Curry Mayo Dipping Sauce: Combine ½ cup mayonnaise, ¼ cup sour cream and ½ teaspoon curry powder in small bowl. Stir in 2 tablespoons minced fresh cilantro.

Cornish Hens with Wild Rice & Pine Nut Pilaf

⅓ cup uncooked wild rice
4 Cornish hens (about 1¼ pounds each)
1 bunch green onions cut into 2-inch pieces
3 tablespoons olive oil, divided
3 tablespoons gluten-free soy sauce
⅓ cup pine nuts
1 cup chopped onion
1 teaspoon dried basil
2 cloves garlic, minced
2 jalapeño peppers,* seeded and minced
½ teaspoon salt
   Black pepper (optional)

Jalapeño peppers can sting and irritate the skin; wear rubber gloves when handling peppers and do not touch your eyes.

1. Preheat oven to 425°F. Cook rice according to package directions.

2. Stuff hens equally with green onions; place hens on rack in roasting pan. Roast 15 minutes. Meanwhile, combine 1 tablespoon oil and soy sauce in small bowl. Baste hens with 1 tablespoon soy sauce mixture; roast 15 minutes or until cooked through (165°F). Baste with remaining soy sauce mixture. Let stand 15 minutes.

3. Heat large skillet over medium-high heat; add pine nuts. Cook 2 minutes or until golden, stirring constantly. Transfer to plate.

4. Add 1 tablespoon oil, onion and basil to same skillet. Cook and stir 5 minutes or until browned. Add garlic; cook and stir 15 seconds. Remove from heat. Add rice, pine nuts, jalapeño peppers, remaining 1 tablespoon oil and salt. Season with black pepper; toss gently to blend. Serve hens with rice mixture. *Makes 4 servings*

Chicken with Herbed Cheese

1 tablespoon butter
2 cups chopped fresh shiitake mushrooms
1 large shallot, minced
¼ teaspoon dried thyme
½ teaspoon salt, divided
½ teaspoon black pepper, divided
¼ cup half-and-half
¼ cup reduced-sodium chicken broth
4 boneless skinless chicken breasts, pounded or sliced ¼ inch thick
¼ cup garlic-and-herb spreadable cheese
4 thin slices (4 ounces) ham
1 tablespoon minced Italian parsley

1. Preheat oven to 350°F. Melt butter in medium skillet. Add mushrooms, shallot, thyme, ¼ teaspoon salt and ¼ teaspoon pepper. Cook and stir over medium heat 5 minutes or until mushrooms are tender. Add half-and-half and broth; simmer 5 minutes or until slightly thickened. Pour half of mixture into shallow ovenproof dish.

2. Place chicken breasts on work surface. Spread 1 tablespoon cheese down center of each breast. Top with 1 ham slice. Roll up; place chicken seam side down over mushroom mixture in dish. Sprinkle with remaining ¼ teaspoon salt and ¼ teaspoon pepper. Top with remaining mushroom mixture. Bake 20 to 25 minutes or until cooked through. Sprinkle with parsley.

Makes 4 servings

Indian-Style Apricot Chicken

6 chicken thighs
¼ teaspoon salt
¼ teaspoon black pepper
1 tablespoon vegetable oil
1 large onion, chopped
2 tablespoons grated fresh ginger
2 cloves garlic, minced
½ teaspoon ground cinnamon
⅛ teaspoon ground allspice
1 can (14½ ounces) diced tomatoes, undrained
1 cup chicken broth
1 package (8 ounces) dried apricots
1 pinch saffron threads (optional)
   Hot basmati rice
2 tablespoons chopped fresh parsley (optional)

Slow Cooker Directions

1. Coat slow cooker with nonstick cooking spray. Season chicken with salt and pepper. Heat oil in large skillet over medium-high heat; brown chicken on all sides. Transfer to slow cooker.

2. Add onion to skillet. Cook and stir 3 to 5 minutes or until translucent. Stir in ginger, garlic, cinnamon and allspice. Cook and stir 15 to 30 seconds or until mixture is fragrant. Add tomatoes with juice and broth. Cook 2 to 3 minutes or until mixture is heated through. Pour into slow cooker.

3. Add apricots and saffron, if desired. Cover; cook on LOW 5 to 6 hours or on HIGH 3 to 3½ hours or until chicken is tender. Serve with basmati rice and garnish with parsley.   *Makes 4 to 6 servings*

Turkey with Pecan-Cherry Stuffing

1 fresh or frozen boneless turkey breast (about 3 to 4 pounds)
2 cups cooked rice
⅓ cup chopped pecans
⅓ cup dried cherries or cranberries
1 teaspoon poultry seasoning
¼ cup peach, apricot or plum preserves
1 teaspoon Worcestershire sauce

Slow Cooker Directions

1. Thaw turkey breast, if frozen. Remove and discard skin. Cut slices three fourths of the way through turkey at 1-inch intervals.

2. Stir together rice, pecans, cherries and poultry seasoning in large bowl. Stuff rice mixture between slices. If needed, skewer turkey lengthwise to hold it together.

3. Place turkey in slow cooker. Cover; cook on LOW 5 to 6 hours or until turkey registers 165°F on meat thermometer inserted into thickest part of breast, not touching stuffing.

4. Stir together preserves and Worcestershire sauce. Spoon over turkey. Cover; let stand 5 minutes. *Makes 8 servings*

Serving Suggestion: Serve with asparagus spears and a spinach salad.

Indian-Inspired Chicken with Raita

Chicken
- **1 cup plain yogurt**
- **2 cloves garlic, minced**
- **1 teaspoon salt**
- **1 teaspoon ground coriander**
- **1 teaspoon ground ginger**
- **½ teaspoon ground turmeric**
- **½ teaspoon ground cinnamon**
- **½ teaspoon ground cumin**
- **¼ teaspoon ground red pepper**
- **1 (5- to 6-pound) chicken, cut into 8 pieces (about 4 pounds chicken parts)**

Raita
- **2 medium cucumbers (about 1 pound), peeled, seeded and thinly sliced**
- **⅓ cup plain yogurt**
- **2 tablespoons chopped fresh cilantro**
- **1 clove garlic, minced**
- **¼ teaspoon salt**
- **⅛ teaspoon black pepper**

1. For chicken, combine yogurt, garlic, salt, coriander, ginger, turmeric, cinnamon, cumin and red pepper in medium bowl. Place chicken in large resealable food storage bag. Add yogurt mixture; marinate in refrigerator 4 to 24 hours, turning occasionally.

2. Preheat broiler. Cover baking sheet with foil. Place chicken on prepared baking sheet. Broil 6 inches from heat about 30 minutes or until cooked through (165°F), turning once.

3. Meanwhile, prepare Raita. Combine cucumbers, yogurt, cilantro, garlic, salt and pepper in large bowl. Serve with chicken.

Makes 6 to 8 servings

South American Chicken & Quinoa

Tomato-Apricot Chutney (page 111)
1 teaspoon ground turmeric
1 teaspoon dried thyme
¾ teaspoon salt, divided
1 pound boneless skinless chicken breasts, cut into 1-inch pieces
2 tablespoons olive oil, divided
1 large green bell pepper, chopped
1 medium onion, chopped
1 cup uncooked quinoa
1 cup chicken broth
1 cup unsweetened coconut milk
1 teaspoon curry powder
¼ teaspoon ground ginger

1. Prepare Tomato-Apricot Chutney; set aside.

2. Combine turmeric, thyme and ¼ teaspoon salt in shallow dish. Dip chicken pieces into spice mixture, coating all sides; set aside.

3. Heat 1 tablespoon oil in large skillet over medium-high heat. Add bell pepper and onion. Cook and stir 2 minutes or until vegetables are crisp-tender. Remove from skillet with slotted spoon; set aside.

4. Add remaining 1 tablespoon oil to skillet. Add chicken pieces. Cook and stir 5 minutes or until browned and chicken is cooked through.

5. Rinse quinoa in fine-mesh strainer under cold running water; drain well.

6. Combine quinoa, chicken broth, coconut milk, curry, remaining ½ teaspoon salt and ginger in large saucepan. Bring to a boil over high heat. Reduce heat to low; simmer, covered, 10 minutes.

7. Stir in chicken and pepper mixture; cook 5 minutes or until liquid is absorbed. Serve with Tomato-Apricot Chutney. *Makes 4 servings*

Tomato-Apricot Chutney

¾ cup apple cider or apple juice
¾ cup finely diced dried apricots
½ cup currants or golden raisins
3 to 4 tablespoons cider vinegar
1 can (about 14 ounces) diced tomatoes, drained
1 tablespoon dark brown sugar
1 teaspoon ground ginger
⅛ teaspoon ground cloves

1. Combine apple cider, apricots, currants and vinegar in small saucepan. Bring to a boil over high heat. Reduce heat to low; simmer, covered, 10 minutes.

2. Stir in tomatoes, brown sugar, ginger and cloves; simmer, uncovered, 5 minutes or until liquid is absorbed. *Makes about 3 cups*

Pesto-Coated Baked Chicken

1 pound boneless skinless chicken cutlets (½ inch thick)
¼ cup plus 1 tablespoon prepared pesto
1½ teaspoons sour cream
1½ teaspoons mayonnaise
1 tablespoon shredded Parmesan cheese
1 tablespoon pine nuts

1. Preheat oven to 450°F. Arrange chicken in single layer in shallow baking pan. Combine pesto, sour cream and mayonnaise in small cup. Brush over chicken. Sprinkle with cheese and pine nuts.

2. Bake 8 to 10 minutes or until chicken is no longer pink in center.
Makes 4 servings

Lemon-Ginger Chicken with Puffed Rice Noodles

Vegetable oil for frying
4 ounces rice noodles, broken in half
3 boneless skinless chicken breasts, cut into strips
1 stalk lemongrass, cut into 1-inch pieces*
3 cloves garlic, minced
1 teaspoon finely chopped fresh ginger
¼ teaspoon ground red pepper
¼ teaspoon black pepper
¼ cup water
1 tablespoon cornstarch
2 tablespoons peanut oil
6 ounces fresh snow peas, trimmed
1 can (8¾ ounces) baby corn, drained and rinsed
¼ cup chopped fresh cilantro
2 tablespoons packed brown sugar
2 tablespoons fish sauce
1 tablespoon gluten-free soy sauce

Or substitute 1½ teaspoons grated lemon peel.

1. Heat 3 inches vegetable oil in wok or Dutch oven until oil registers 375°F on deep-fry thermometer. Fry noodles in small batches 20 seconds or until puffy, holding down noodles in oil with slotted spoon to fry evenly. Drain on paper towels; set aside.

2. Combine chicken, lemongrass, garlic, ginger, red pepper and black pepper in medium bowl. Combine water and cornstarch in small bowl; set aside.

3. Heat wok over high heat 1 minute. Drizzle peanut oil into wok and heat 30 seconds. Add chicken mixture; stir-fry 3 minutes or until cooked through.

4. Add snow peas and baby corn; stir-fry 1 to 2 minutes. Stir cornstarch mixture; add to wok. Cook 1 minute or until thickened.

5. Add cilantro, brown sugar, fish sauce and soy sauce; cook until heated through. Discard lemongrass. Serve over rice noodles.

Makes 4 servings

Turkey Piccata

2½ tablespoons rice flour
¼ teaspoon salt
¼ teaspoon black pepper
1 pound turkey breast, cut into short strips*
1 tablespoon butter
1 tablespoon olive oil
½ cup chicken broth
Grated peel of 1 lemon
2 teaspoons lemon juice
2 tablespoons finely chopped parsley
2 cups cooked rice

Or substitute turkey tenderloins.

Slow Cooker Directions

1. Combine rice flour, salt and pepper in resealable food storage bag. Add turkey strips and shake well to coat. Heat butter and oil in large skillet over medium-high heat. Add turkey strips in single layer. Brown on all sides, about 2 minutes per side. Arrange in single layer in slow cooker.

2. Pour broth into skillet. Cook and stir to scrape up any browned bits. Pour into slow cooker. Add lemon peel and juice. Cover; cook on LOW 2 hours. Sprinkle with parsley before serving. Serve over rice.

Makes 4 servings

*Tip

It's a shame to limit turkey to Thanksgiving Day. Now that turkey breasts, turkey tenders and other fresh cuts are available all year long, try substituting turkey in your favorite chicken recipe. Turkey is lean, flavorful and an excellent source of protein.

Orange-Almond Chicken

6 boneless skinless chicken breasts
Salt and black pepper
1½ cups sliced almonds
2 tablespoons rice flour
Grated peel of 1 medium orange (about 2 teaspoons)
1 egg
2 tablespoons water
2 to 4 tablespoons olive oil
Juice of 2 medium oranges (about ½ cup)
¾ cup chicken broth
1 tablespoon Dijon mustard
Additional grated orange peel and almonds (optional)

1. Cover chicken breasts with plastic wrap and pound to ¼-inch thickness; season with salt and pepper. Place almonds and rice flour in food processor; process using on/off pulsing action until coarse crumbs form. Add orange peel and pulse to combine.

2. Lightly beat egg and water in shallow bowl. Place almond mixture on plate. Coat chicken breasts in egg and then in almond mixture, pressing to make almond coating stick.

3. Heat 2 tablespoons oil in large skillet over medium-high heat. Cook chicken in batches without crowding skillet until lightly browned and no longer pink in center, about 5 minutes per side. Keep warm.

4. Add orange juice to same skillet; cook and stir until reduced by about half, scraping up brown bits on bottom of skillet. Add chicken broth and mustard; cook and stir 2 to 3 minutes. Pour over chicken. Garnish with additional orange peel and almonds, if desired. *Makes 6 servings*

Serving Suggestion: Serve on a bed of buttered French-cut green beans.

Creole Vegetables & Chicken

1 can (about 14 ounces) diced tomatoes
8 ounces frozen cut okra
2 cups chopped green bell peppers
1 cup chopped onions
1 cup reduced-sodium chicken broth
¾ cup sliced celery
2 teaspoons Worcestershire sauce
1 teaspoon dried thyme
1 bay leaf
1 tablespoon olive oil
1 pound chicken tenders, cut into bite-size pieces
1½ teaspoons sugar
¾ teaspoon Cajun seasoning
   Hot pepper sauce (optional)
¼ cup chopped fresh parsley

Slow Cooker Directions

1. Coat slow cooker with nonstick cooking spray. Add tomatoes, okra, bell peppers, onions, broth, celery, Worcestershire sauce, thyme and bay leaf. Cover; cook on LOW 9 hours or on HIGH 4½ hours.

2. Heat oil in large skillet over medium-high heat. Add chicken; cook and stir 6 minutes or until lightly browned. Add chicken, sugar, Cajun seasoning and hot pepper sauce, if desired, to slow cooker. *Increase slow cooker temperature to HIGH.* Cook, uncovered, on HIGH 15 minutes. Add parsley. *Makes 4 servings*

Note: The frozen okra does not have to be thawed in this recipe. The okra helps to thicken the dish without adding flour.

Spicy Roasted Chickpeas (p. 136)

Flourless Peanut Butter Cookies (p. 122)

Citrus Tapioca Pudding
(p. 130)

Mixed Berry Crisp
(p. 132)

Snacks & Treats

Flourless Peanut Butter Cookies

1 cup packed light brown sugar
1 cup smooth peanut butter
1 egg, lightly beaten
½ cup semisweet chocolate chips, melted

1. Preheat oven to 350°F. Beat brown sugar, peanut butter and egg in medium bowl with electric mixer until blended and smooth.

2. Shape dough into 24 balls; place 2 inches apart on ungreased cookie sheets. Flatten slightly with fork. Bake 10 to 12 minutes or until set. Transfer to wire rack; cool completely. Drizzle with chocolate.

Makes about 2 dozen cookies

Flourless Almond Cookies

1 cup sugar
1 cup almond butter
1 egg, lightly beaten

1. Preheat oven to 350°F. Beat sugar, almond butter and egg in large bowl with electric mixer until well combined.

2. Shape dough into 24 balls; place 2 inches apart on ungreased cookie sheets. Flatten slightly with fork.

3. Bake 10 minutes or until set. Transfer to wire rack; cool completely.

Makes about 2 dozen cookies

Cranberry-Orange Rice Pudding

1 cup uncooked rice*
1 tablespoon grated orange peel
1½ cups dried cranberries, coarsely chopped
½ cup orange juice
1 quart (4 cups) milk
1 can (12 ounces) evaporated milk
⅔ cup sugar
⅛ teaspoon salt

1½ cups parboiled quick-cooking rice or 3 cups cooked rice can be substituted.

1. Cook rice according to package directions adding orange peel.

2. Meanwhile, combine cranberries and orange juice in medium saucepan; bring to a simmer over medium heat. Simmer 7 minutes or until juice is absorbed. Set aside.

3. Add milk, evaporated milk, sugar and salt to cooked rice. Cook and stir over medium-low heat about 40 minutes or until slightly thickened.

4. Stir cranberries into rice mixture. Cool to room temperature. Cover; refrigerate. Let stand at room temperature 10 minutes before serving.

Makes 8 servings

*Tip

Chances are, if your diet is gluten-free you're eating more rice. It's a tasty carbohydrate that can fill in for flour-based pastas and starches. It's a great opportunity to enjoy some of the many different kinds of rice now readily available. Your supermarket probably stocks brown rice, basmati rice, long grain rice, jasmine rice and others.

Almond Flour Pound Cake

½ cup (1 stick) butter, softened
½ cup cream cheese, softened
¾ cup sugar
4 eggs
1 teaspoon vanilla
2 cups almond flour*
1 teaspoon baking powder
½ teaspoon salt
¼ teaspoon ground ginger
¼ teaspoon ground cardamom
1 tablespoon honey roasted sliced almonds
Berries and whipped cream (optional)

Almond flour, also called almond meal, is available at natural foods stores and in the specialty flour section at many supermarkets.

1. Preheat oven to 350°F. Spray 9×5-inch loaf pan (or 2 mini loaf pans) with nonstick cooking spray.

2. Beat butter, cream cheese and sugar in large bowl with electric mixer until well blended.

3. Add eggs, one at a time, beating after each addition. Beat in vanilla.

4. Combine almond flour, baking powder, salt, ginger and cardamom in medium bowl. Gradually add to egg mixture while beating on medium speed.

5. Pour into prepared pan; sprinkle with sliced almonds. Bake 45 to 55 minutes or until toothpick inserted into center comes out clean. Serve with berries and whipped cream, if desired.   *Makes 9 (1-inch) slices*

Falafel Nuggets

Falafel
  2 cans (15 ounces each) chickpeas, rinsed and drained
  ½ cup rice flour
  ½ cup chopped fresh parsley
  1 egg
    Juice of 1 lemon
  ¼ cup minced onion
  2 tablespoons minced garlic
  2 teaspoons ground cumin
  ½ teaspoon salt
  ½ teaspoon ground red pepper or red pepper flakes
  ½ cup canola oil

Sauce
  2½ cups tomato sauce
  ⅓ cup tomato paste
  2 tablespoons lemon juice
  2 teaspoons sugar
  1 teaspoon dry onion powder
  ½ teaspoon salt

1. Preheat oven to 400°F. Coat baking sheet with nonstick cooking spray.

2. Combine chickpeas, rice flour, parsley, egg, lemon juice, minced onion, garlic, cumin, ½ teaspoon salt and red pepper in food processor or blender; process until well blended. Shape mixture into 1-inch balls.

3. For sauce, combine tomato sauce, tomato paste, lemon juice, sugar, onion powder and salt in medium saucepan. Simmer over medium-low heat 20 minutes; keep warm.

4. Heat oil in large nonstick skillet over medium-high heat. Fry falafel in batches until browned. Place 2 inches apart on baking sheet; bake 8 to 10 minutes. Serve with warm sauce. *Makes 12 servings*

Hint: Falafel also can be baked completely to reduce fat content. Spray balls lightly with nonstick cooking spray and bake 15 to 20 minutes, turning once.

Citrus Tapioca Pudding

    2 navel oranges
    ⅓ cup sugar
    3 tablespoons quick-cooking tapioca
 2½ cups milk
    1 egg, lightly beaten
    ½ teaspoon almond extract
      Ground cinnamon or nutmeg
      Orange slices (optional)

1. Grate peel of 1 orange into medium saucepan. Add sugar, tapioca, milk and egg; let stand 5 minutes. Cook and stir over medium heat 5 minutes or until mixture comes to a boil. Remove from heat; stir in almond extract. Cool, uncovered, 20 minutes. Stir well; let cool to room temperature. Refrigerate, covered, at least 2 hours.

2. Peel and dice oranges. Stir tapioca mixture; fold in oranges. Spoon evenly into 8 dessert dishes. Sprinkle each serving with cinnamon; garnish with orange slices, if desired. *Makes 8 servings*

Parmesan Sage Crisps

 1½ cups (about 4 ounces) shredded Parmesan cheese*
    2 to 3 tablespoons finely chopped fresh sage leaves
    ½ teaspoon black pepper

Do not use finely grated cheese for this recipe.

1. Preheat oven to 350°F. Line baking sheets with parchment paper.

2. Combine cheese, sage and pepper in medium bowl; mix well. Place scant ⅓ cup cheese mixture on prepared baking sheet; spread into 5-inch circle. Repeat with remaining cheese mixture.

3. Bake 7 to 8 minutes or just until lightly browned. Cool on baking sheets about 2 minutes. When cool enough to handle, peel cheese crisps from paper. Cool completely. Cut circles into pieces. *Makes 8 servings*

Mixed Berry Crisp

6 cups mixed berries, thawed if frozen
¾ cup packed brown sugar, divided
¼ cup quick-cooking tapioca
   Juice of ½ lemon
1 teaspoon ground cinnamon
6 tablespoons cold butter, cut into pieces
½ cup rice flour
½ cup sliced almonds

1. Preheat oven to 375°F. Grease sides and bottom of 8- or 9-inch square baking pan.

2. Place berries in large bowl. Add ¼ cup sugar, tapioca, lemon juice and cinnamon; stir until well combined. Let stand while preparing topping.

3. Place butter, remaining ½ cup sugar and rice flour in food processor. Pulse until coarse crumbs form. Add almonds; pulse until combined. (Leave some large pieces of almonds.)

4. Transfer berry mixture to prepared pan. Sprinkle topping over berries. Bake 20 to 30 minutes or until topping is browned and filling is bubbly.

Makes about 9 servings

*Tip

For a gluten-free fruit dessert, a crisp is considerably easier than a pie since you don't need to bother with making a special crust. This recipe uses quick-cooking tapioca as a thickening agent, but you could also use cornstarch or arrowroot.

Flourless Chocolate Cake

1 cup whipping cream
1 cup plus 2 tablespoons sugar
12 squares (1 ounce each) unsweetened chocolate, coarsely chopped
4 squares (1 ounce each) semisweet chocolate, coarsely chopped
6 eggs, at room temperature
½ cup strong coffee
¼ teaspoon salt
½ cup chopped walnuts, divided
1 cup whipped cream (optional)

1. Set oven rack to middle position. Preheat oven to 350°F. Spray 8-inch round cake pan with nonstick cooking spray.

2. Beat cream with 2 tablespoons sugar in large bowl with electric mixer at high speed until soft peaks form; set aside.

3. Place unsweetened and semisweet chocolate in large microwavable bowl; microwave on HIGH 2 to 3 minutes or until chocolate is melted, stirring after 1 minute and at 30-second intervals after the first minute.

4. Beat eggs and remaining 1 cup sugar in large bowl with electric mixer at high speed about 7 minutes or until pale and thick. Add melted chocolate, coffee and salt to egg mixture; beat until well blended.

5. Fold whipped cream and ¼ cup walnuts into egg mixture. Spread in prepared pan; sprinkle with remaining ¼ cup walnuts. Place pan in large roasting pan; add enough hot water to roasting pan to reach halfway up side of pan. Bake 30 to 35 minutes or until set but still soft in center.

6. To unmold, loosen edge of cake with knife; place serving plate upside down over pan and invert. Serve warm garnished with whipped cream, if desired.

Makes 12 servings

Spicy Roasted Chickpeas

1 can (about 20 ounces) chickpeas
3 tablespoons olive oil
½ teaspoon salt
½ teaspoon black pepper
¾ to 1 tablespoon chili powder
⅛ to ¼ teaspoon ground red pepper
1 lime, cut into wedges

1. Preheat oven to 400°F. Rinse chickpeas in colander; drain well, shaking colander to remove as much water as possible.

2. Combine chickpeas, olive oil, salt and black pepper in large bowl. Spread chickpeas in single layer in 15×10-inch baking pan. Bake 15 minutes or until chickpeas begin to brown, shaking pan twice during baking.

3. Sprinkle with chili powder and red pepper to taste; bake 5 minutes or until dark golden-red. Serve with lime wedges. *Makes 4 servings*

Snack Mix

3 cups gluten-free rice cereal squares
3 cups popped popcorn
½ cup mixed nuts or peanuts
3 tablespoons vegetable oil
⅓ cup grated Parmesan cheese
2 teaspoons garlic salt
2 teaspoons chili powder

1. Preheat oven to 350°F. Combine cereal, popcorn and nuts in large bowl. Drizzle with oil and stir to coat. Sprinkle with cheese, garlic salt and chili powder, stirring to coat evenly.

2. Spread mixture on large ungreased baking sheet. Bake 15 minutes, turning pan once. Store in airtight container. *Makes about 6 servings*

Chocolate Coconut Almond Macaroons

1⅓ cups flaked sweetened coconut (3½-ounce can)
⅔ cup sugar
2 egg whites
½ teaspoon vanilla
¼ teaspoon almond extract
   Pinch salt
4 ounces sliced almonds, coarsely crushed
20 whole almonds
   Chocolate Ganache (recipe follows)

1. Combine coconut, sugar, egg whites, vanilla, almond extract and salt in medium bowl; mix well. Fold in sliced almonds. Cover and refrigerate at least 1 hour or overnight.

2. Preheat oven to 350°F. Line baking sheet with parchment paper. Roll dough by tablespoonfuls into balls. Place 1 inch apart on prepared sheet. Press almond on top of each cookie. Bake 15 minutes or until light brown. Cool cookies 5 minutes on baking sheet. Transfer to wire rack; cool completely.

3. Meanwhile, prepare Chocolate Ganache. Let ganache cool 10 to 15 minutes.

4. Dip bottom of each cookie into ganache. Place cookies on clean parchment or waxed paper-lined baking sheet. Refrigerate until ganache is firm. Store covered in refrigerator.   *Makes 1½ dozen cookies*

Chocolate Ganache: Place ½ cup semisweet chocolate chips in shallow bowl. Heat ¼ cup whipping cream in small saucepan until bubbles form around edges. Pour cream over chocolate; let stand 5 minutes. Stir until smooth.

VOLUME MEASUREMENTS (dry)

1/8 teaspoon = 0.5 mL
1/4 teaspoon = 1 mL
1/2 teaspoon = 2 mL
3/4 teaspoon = 4 mL
1 teaspoon = 5 mL
1 tablespoon = 15 mL
2 tablespoons = 30 mL
1/4 cup = 60 mL
1/3 cup = 75 mL
1/2 cup = 125 mL
2/3 cup = 150 mL
3/4 cup = 175 mL
1 cup = 250 mL
2 cups = 1 pint = 500 mL
3 cups = 750 mL
4 cups = 1 quart = 1 L

VOLUME MEASUREMENTS (fluid)

1 fluid ounce (2 tablespoons) = 30 mL
4 fluid ounces (1/2 cup) = 125 mL
8 fluid ounces (1 cup) = 250 mL
12 fluid ounces (1 1/2 cups) = 375 mL
16 fluid ounces (2 cups) = 500 mL

WEIGHTS (mass)

1/2 ounce = 15 g
1 ounce = 30 g
3 ounces = 90 g
4 ounces = 120 g
8 ounces = 225 g
10 ounces = 285 g
12 ounces = 360 g
16 ounces = 1 pound = 450 g

DIMENSIONS

1/16 inch = 2 mm
1/8 inch = 3 mm
1/4 inch = 6 mm
1/2 inch = 1.5 cm
3/4 inch = 2 cm
1 inch = 2.5 cm

OVEN TEMPERATURES

250°F = 120°C
275°F = 140°C
300°F = 150°C
325°F = 160°C
350°F = 180°C
375°F = 190°C
400°F = 200°C
425°F = 220°C
450°F = 230°C

BAKING PAN SIZES

Utensil	Size in Inches/Quarts	Metric Volume	Size in Centimeters
Baking or Cake Pan (square or rectangular)	8×8×2	2 L	20×20×5
	9×9×2	2.5 L	23×23×5
	12×8×2	3 L	30×20×5
	13×9×2	3.5 L	33×23×5
Loaf Pan	8×4×3	1.5 L	20×10×7
	9×5×3	2 L	23×13×7
Round Layer Cake Pan	8×1½	1.2 L	20×4
	9×1½	1.5 L	23×4
Pie Plate	8×1¼	750 mL	20×3
	9×1¼	1 L	23×3
Baking Dish or Casserole	1 quart	1 L	—
	1½ quart	1.5 L	—
	2 quart	2 L	—